RIDDLES TO TELL
YOUR CAT

BY CAROLINE LEVINE
PICTURES BY MEYER SELTZER

THAT WAS A GOOD ONE. TELL ME ANOTHER!

Albert Whitman & Company, Morton Grove, Illinois

Library of Congress Cataloging-in-Publication Data

Levine, Caroline Anne.
  Riddles to tell your cat / Caroline Levine ;
illustrated by Meyer Seltzer.
      p.   cm.
  Summary: A collection of jokes, riddles, and
tales about cats.
  ISBN 0-8075-7006-0
  1. Riddles, Juvenile.   2. Cats—Juvenile
humor.   3. Wit and humor, Juvenile.
[1. Cats—Wit and humor.   2. Riddles.   3. Jokes.]
I.   Seltzer, Meyer, ill.   II. Title.
PN6371.5.L45   1992
818'.5402—dc20   91-36492
                                         CIP
                                         AC

Published in 1992 by Albert Whitman & Company,
6340 Oakton Street, Morton Grove, Illinois 60053-2723.
Published simultaneously in Canada by
General Publishing, Limited, Toronto.

For Karen, my kitten. C.L.

For Katchen, Munchkin, Frida,
and in fond memory of Rumbles. M.S.

Culinary Cats

What do cats eat for breakfast?
Mice Krispies.

What happened to the Siamese who ate lemons
for breakfast?
She turned into a sour-puss.

What is a cat's favorite jam?
Orange meow-malade.

Where do young cats learn to cook?
In the kit-chen.

What does a lion like to eat
in a restaurant?
The waitress.

What do cats do after a big meal?
They purr-p.

What does a beagle put on his hamburger?
Cat-sup, of course.

Mama Tiger: What are you doing?
Child Tiger: I'm chasing a hunter around
the tree.
Mama Tiger: I've told you a million times
not to play with your food!

Feline Fashion

SQUEEKY CLEAN
WHILE YOU'RE AWAY
WE WORK NOT PLAY

WE CAN FIX IT, SIR!

Why was the leopard unhappy with
the cleaners?
Because they took out all his spots.

Where do pussycats buy their clothes?
From cat-alogs.

Why can a tomcat leave home in a hurry?
He doesn't have to waste time putting on his coat.

Why was the kitten born wearing a sweater?
Her mama had swallowed a ball of yarn.

What kind of diapers do mother cats buy?
Pam-purrs.

Why did the boy take the harness off his cat?
It was the leash he could do.

Cool School Cats

What kind of math do cats do well?
Figuring purr-cents.

What is a cat's favorite subject in school?
Meow-sic.

Cat Teacher: Kitty, please spell the
word "enemy."
Kitty: D-O-G.

Feline University
confers
the Degree
of
V.S.C.
(Very Smart Cat)
to
Ting-Ting

How did the Siamese prove that she
had gone to college?
She showed everyone her pet-degree.

What's the difference between a cat
and a comma?
*A cat shows claws at the ends of its paws,
and a comma shows a pause at the end
of a clause.*

Why did the teacher fail the cat?
Because he was a cheetah.

I'M OUTTA HERE!

A "MOUSETRAP" MAJOR!

Stink Pinks

What would you call a vampire kitten?
A bat cat.

What is a cat's sore foot?
A raw paw.

What do you call talk between two lions?
Cat chat.

What do cats use to season their rodents?
Mice spice.

What do you call an ill-mannered feline?
A cat brat.

What is a cougar's cushion?
A cat mat.

STINKIE PINKS?

NO, NO... STINK PINKS ARE ONE-SYLLABLE WORDS, AND STINKIE PINKIES, HAVE TWO SYLLABLES.

Stinkie Pinkies

What do you call cats falling from the sky
in winter?
A furry flurry.

What is a cat who talks a lot?
A gabby tabby.

What do you call a young cat in love?
A smitten kitten.

What is an out-of-shape cat?
A flabby tabby.

What does a young cat wear to keep
her paws warm?
Kitten mittens.

What do you call a raggedy striped cat?
A shabby tabby.

E-meow-gency Room

Why did the alley cat visit a clock doctor?
Because he had ticks.

Why did the tomcat see a psychiatrist?
Because he had an Oedi-puss complex.

How did the doctor examine the panther's brain?
She used a CAT scan.

What did the tabby say when the doctor
gave her a shot?
Me-<u>ow</u>!

What did the doctor put on the lion's poison ivy?
Cat-amine lotion.

Why did the calico have to go to the eye doctor?
To have his cat-aracts removed.

LOOK AT THE
SCAREDY CAT!

Cat Tales

Ann: I lost my cat last week.
Dan: Did you put an ad in the paper?
Ann: No, dummy. My cat can't read!

Five copycats were sitting on a fence.
One jumped off. How many were left?
None.

Knock, knock.
Who's there?
Cattle.
Cattle, who?
Cattle always purr when you pet her.

Jim: Why are you feeding birdseed to my cat?
Kim: Because that's where my bird is!

If a lion and a turtle escape from the zoo,
which one should you try to catch first?
The lion—that's the mane thing.

Knock, knock.
Who's there?
Ocelot.
Ocelot, who?
You oc-e-lot
of questions!

Career Cats

Why did the skyscraper builder hire cougars?
Because they weren't afraid to use the cat-walks.

Why do cats make good lifeguards?
They know how to give mouse-to-mouse resuscitation.

Who does the government send
to foreign countries?
A diplo-cat.

Why did the cat always ride with the ambulance?
He was their first-aid kit.

Why was the policecat a good musician?
She was always on the beat.

Why was the striped cat such a good accountant?
Because he could tab-ulate so fast.

What kind of cat doesn't need a career?
An aristo-cat.

Crazy Cat Crosses

What do you get when you cross a kitten
with a post?
A caterpillar.

What do you get when you cross a drum
with a male tabby?
A tom-tom cat.

What do you get when you cross a cat
with a laughing hyena?
A gigglepuss.

What do you get when you cross a leopard
with a cottage?
A house cat.

What do you get when you cross a cat
with galoshes?
Puss-in-boots.

What do you get when you cross a lion with a canary?
I don't know—but if it sings, you'd better listen.

Relax, Cat!

What kind of car does a wealthy cat drive?
A Cat-illac.

What did the collie worry about when planning
a surprise party?
That somebody would let the cat out of the bag.

What happened when the cougar tried to go sailing?
It was a cat-astrophe.

What do felines grow in their gardens?
Pussywillows, cattails, and tiger lilies.

Where do pumas vacation?
In the Cat-skill Mountains.

What is a cat's idea of a
perfect evening?
A little catnip followed by a catnap.

Meow-sic & Litter-ature

How does a cat keep her place in a book?
She dog-ears the page.

What well-known piano piece did Beethoven
write for his cat?
Für Elise.

Why did the cat tell the girl a joke?
He wanted to a-mews her.

Where do most cats play in the orchestra?
In the purr-cussion section.

Why did the Persian tell his kittens a tall tale?
Because he loved to spin a yarn.

Which rock group do cool cats love?
The New Kits on the Block.

Purry Poems

There once were two cats of Kilkenny.
Each thought there was one cat too many.
So they fought and they fit,
And they scratched and they bit
Till, excepting their nails
And the tips of their tails,
Instead of two cats, there weren't any.

Anonymous

The funniest thing I've ever seen
Was a tomcat sewing on a sewing machine.
Oh, the sewing machine got running too slow,
And it took seven stitches in the tomcat's toe.

Anonymous

WELCOME TO
KILKENNY
POP. 0

There was a young man from the city
Who met what he thought was a kitty.
He gave it a pat
And said, "Nice little cat!"
(They buried his clothes out of pity.)
Anonymous

Ashes to ashes
And dust to dust,
Show me a cat
That a mouse can trust.
Anonymous

There was a young lady of Niger
Who smiled as she rode on a tiger.
They returned from the ride
With the lady inside,
And the smile on the face of the tiger.
Anonymous

R.I.P.
Young
Man
from the
City

Famous Felines

Who really was the first to fly a plane?
Kitty Hawk.

What football team roars when
it scores a touchdown?
The Detroit Lions.

Who was Egypt's most beautiful queen?
Cleo-cat-ra.

What baseball team is afraid of cats?
The Toronto Blue Jays.

Kitty-days

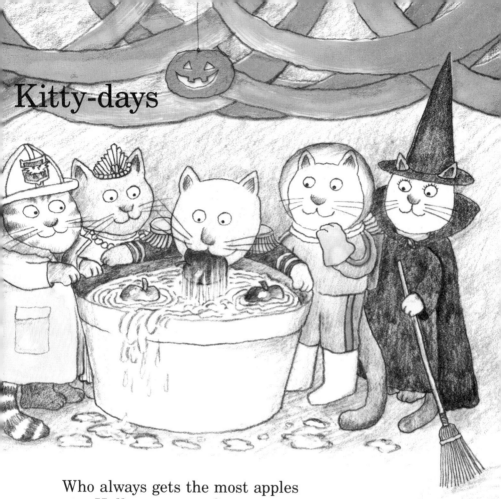

Who always gets the most apples
at a Halloween party?
The bobcat.

What do cats kiss under at Christmas parties?
Mouseltoe.

What do cats say on Valentine's Day?
"Will you be mine, feline?"

Who do kittens want to see on Christmas Eve?
Santa Claws.

Mousellaneous

What did the five-hundred-pound parrot
say to the cat?
"Here, kitty, kitty, kitty."

What do you call a cat in disguise?
An im-purr-sonator.

How does a zoologist group cats?
She puts them in cat-egories.

Why did the sergeant salute the tiger?
The tiger had more stripes.

What card game do cats like to play?
Go Fish.

Why did the cat get in trouble for bragging?
Because he was lion.

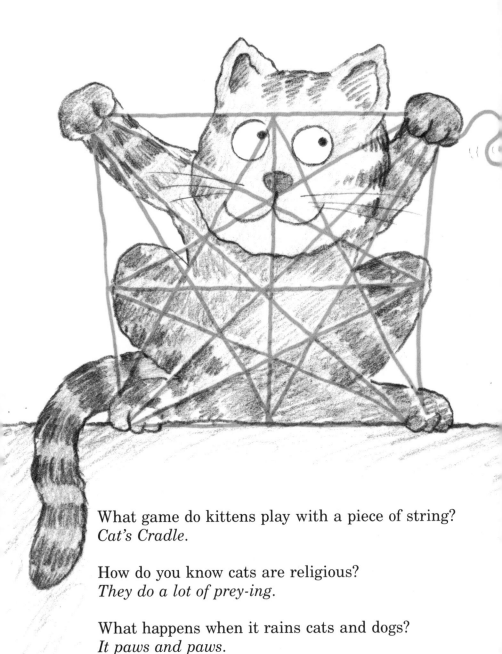

What game do kittens play with a piece of string?
Cat's Cradle.

How do you know cats are religious?
They do a lot of prey-ing.

What happens when it rains cats and dogs?
It paws and paws.

Why did the cat wish he were a frog?
A frog has more than nine lives—
it croaks every night.

What did the Romans use to style their hair?
Cat-a-combs.

How do cats get married?
They exchange wedding meows.

Why couldn't the alley cat make up her mind?
She was always sitting on the fence.

What do you call an eight-sided cat?
An octo-puss.

Why do people love cats so much?
Because they have lots of purr-sonality.